Performance Measurement

Md. Shohidul Islam

Performance Measurement and Improvement of TCP

An In-Depth Performance Analysis of TCP Over Wired and Wireless Network Using NS-2

VDM Verlag Dr. Müller

Impressum/Imprint (nur für Deutschland/ only for Germany)

Bibliografische Information der Deutschen Nationalbibliothek: Die Deutsche Nationalbibliothek verzeichnet diese Publikation in der Deutschen Nationalbibliografie; detaillierte bibliografische Daten sind im Internet über http://dnb.d-nb.de abrufbar.
Alle in diesem Buch genannten Marken und Produktnamen unterliegen warenzeichen-, marken- oder patentrechtlichem Schutz bzw. sind Warenzeichen oder eingetragene Warenzeichen der jeweiligen Inhaber. Die Wiedergabe von Marken, Produktnamen, Gebrauchsnamen, Handelsnamen, Warenbezeichnungen u.s.w. in diesem Werk berechtigt auch ohne besondere Kennzeichnung nicht zu der Annahme, dass solche Namen im Sinne der Warenzeichen- und Markenschutzgesetzgebung als frei zu betrachten wären und daher von jedermann benutzt werden dürften.

Coverbild: www.ingimage.com

Verlag: VDM Verlag Dr. Müller Aktiengesellschaft & Co. KG
Dudweiler Landstr. 99, 66123 Saarbrücken, Deutschland
Telefon +49 681 9100-698, Telefax +49 681 9100-988
Email: info@vdm-verlag.de
Zugl.: Bangladesh, Rajshahi University of Engineering & Technology, Diss., 2007

Herstellung in Deutschland:
Schaltungsdienst Lange o.H.G., Berlin
Books on Demand GmbH, Norderstedt
Reha GmbH, Saarbrücken
Amazon Distribution GmbH, Leipzig
ISBN: 978-3-639-26421-0

Imprint (only for USA, GB)

Bibliographic information published by the Deutsche Nationalbibliothek: The Deutsche Nationalbibliothek lists this publication in the Deutsche Nationalbibliografie; detailed bibliographic data are available in the Internet at http://dnb.d-nb.de.
Any brand names and product names mentioned in this book are subject to trademark, brand or patent protection and are trademarks or registered trademarks of their respective holders. The use of brand names, product names, common names, trade names, product descriptions etc. even without a particular marking in this works is in no way to be construed to mean that such names may be regarded as unrestricted in respect of trademark and brand protection legislation and could thus be used by anyone.

Cover image: www.ingimage.com

Publisher: VDM Verlag Dr. Müller Aktiengesellschaft & Co. KG
Dudweiler Landstr. 99, 66123 Saarbrücken, Germany
Phone +49 681 9100-698, Fax +49 681 9100-988
Email: info@vdm-publishing.com

Printed in the U.S.A.
Printed in the U.K. by (see last page)
ISBN: 978-3-639-26421-0

Contents

i

1

Introduction

1.1 TCP/IP Architecture

TCP/IP architecture is composed of basically five interrelated layers. Each upper one works as a preprocessor for its immediate lower layer. Contents of Application file are converted into electrical signal at the time of transferring toward destination. A picture of TCP/IP protocol stack [9] has been shown in Figure 1.1. Each layer performs a specific task. The discussion of this stack has been given from the bottom to up.

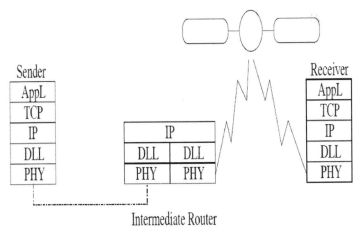

Fig. 1.1 TCP/IP protocol stack

1

The lowest layer is the physical layer (PHY), which represents the physical medium used for communication. A wide range of transmission media can be used, for example coaxial cable, fiber-optic, or twisted pair.

Next is the Data Link Layer (DLL) which is divided into two subs-layers: Medium Access Control (MAC) layer, that controls the access to the physical medium, and Logical Link Control (LLC) layer, that can provide reliable, connection oriented service between two neighboring network elements.

The center piece of the internet protocol stack is the Internet Protocol (IP). It is located on the third (network) layer in the stack. Every computer connected to the Internet needs to run this protocol. There is no alternative. IP is responsible for finding a path through the network from the sending to the receiving end-host, a task called routing. Intermediate nodes, called routers, forward the packets from one hop to the next until the destination is reached. The IP protocol is considered to be unreliable, which means it is allowed to lose or re-order data packets during transmission.

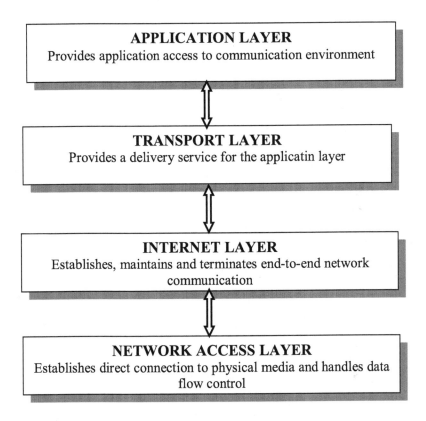

Fig. 1.2 Functions of layers of TCP/IP model

Above the network layer, it is transport layer. This layer generally only exists in end hosts of the Internet, not in the routers. There are two protocols used at the transport layer: User Datagram Protocol (UDP), which is unreliable and only provides addressing to the specific application in the end-computer, and Transmission Control Protocol (TCP), which is a reliable transport protocol.

The highest layer in the Internet protocol stack is the Application layer. In this layer an unlimited variety of application protocols can exist. The most common ones are the World Wide Web (WWW), e-mail and File Transfer Protocol (FTP).

Traditionally the physical media used to interconnect computers have been wire-based. The common characteristics of these media are the very low probability of data loss due to bit errors, the fast transmission of one packet between two end hosts, usually in the millisecond range, and the same bandwidth availability for the forward (sender to receiver) and the return (receiver to sender) path.

1.2 TCP Variants

Transmission Control Protocol includes eleven variants (Tahoe, FullTcp, TCP/Asym, Reno, Reno/Asym, Newreno, Newreno/Asym, Sack1, Fack, Vegas and VegasRBP) as source and five (TCPSink, TCPSink/Asym, Sack1, DelAck and Sack1/DelAck) as destination, implemented in *Network Simulator 2 (NS-2)*.The reason behind the variations of TCP is that each type possesses some special criteria. Such as the base TCP has become known as TCP Tahoe. TCP Reno adds one

4

new mechanism called Fast Recovery to TCP Tahoe. TCP Newreno uses the newest retransmission mechanism of TCP Reno. The use of Sacks permits the receiver to specify several additional data packets that have been received out-of-order within one dupack, instead of only the last in order packet received. TCP Vegas proposes its own unique retransmission and congestion control strategies. TCP Fack is Reno TCP with forward acknowledgment. In recent years the use of non-wire line physical media has become more and more common in computer networks. Wireless networks can support user mobility and can be deployed with much less infrastructure than their wired counterparts. Cellular Mobile System can provide access to users in geographically remote areas, serve as an emergency backup if the wired infrastructure is destroyed, or connect distant network islands. These new media have quite different characteristics to the wired network. The delay between packet transmission and reception can be much higher, because of the long propagation delay of noisy channel. Wireless links are often noisy, which means that packet loss due to bit errors is quite likely. There is also the possibility of different bandwidth on the forward and return channel.

1.3 Motivation

A packet loss is occurred in a wired network mainly due to network congestion. On the other hand in a wireless link, packet losses are caused mainly due to bit errors resulted from noise, interference, and various kind of fading. When TCP detects a packet loss, it assumes this loss is caused by congestion and turns on its congestion control algorithms [20] and eventually slows down the amount of data it transmits to adjust with the low capacity of the network. When a packet is lost, TCP has no idea whether this loss is caused by congestion or bit error. As a result when packets are lost due to bit errors of wireless channel, TCP unwisely interprets these losses as due to congestion and invokes congestion control algorithms, and reduces data transfer rate. This wrong act of TCP makes matters worse.

Incase of noisy channel, traditional wireless TCP has several drawbacks: unwise drop of congestion window, higher retransmission of same packet, lower degree buffer utilization and idle expanses of CPU cycles. As a result TCP throughput degrades drastically. This thesis work has been motivated to resolve these undesired features by one mean: *dynamic packet correction* at destination end, before entering it into the buffer.

2

TCP Background

The Transmission Control Protocol (TCP) is the most commonly used transport layer protocol in the Internet. It provides reliable, end to end, non- real-time data transfer. Since its original specification in 1981 TCP has undergone several changes and enhancements. This chapter will give an overview of the development of TCP, describe the most commonly used versions in to days Internet and introduce some experimental versions investigated in this thesis.

2.1 TCP for Wired Link

2.1.1 *Original TCP*

The use of sequence numbers for TCP is reliability and in-order delivery, and the basic timeout based retransmission strategy. For the unambiguous use of sequence numbers a three-way handshake is needed at connection set-up. This handshake has been shown in Figure 2.1.

It enables a full-duplex data transmission and ensures that no packets from an old connection will be accepted. The original

TCP version also includes a mechanism for flow control that enables a slow receiver to stop a sender from transmitting too fast. Flow control is achieved by the receiver's advertised window in the TCP acknowledgment packets. However it is the basis for all other TCP Variants introduced in the following sections.

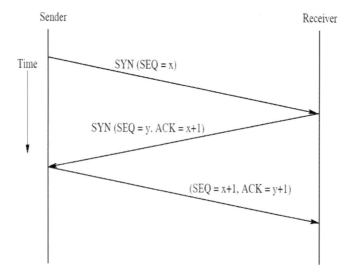

Fig. 2.1 Three-way handshake

2.1.2 *TCP Tahoe*

Two variables are used to achieve congestion control in Tahoe: the congestion window (cwnd) and the slow start threshold (ssthresh) [9]. The congestion window governs the amount of data a connection is currently allowed to transmit, while the

8

slow start threshold determines in which phase of the congestion control procedure the connection is currently in. Tahoe's congestion control mechanism consists of two phases: Slow Start, which is executed at the beginning of the connection and after every packet loss, and Congestion Avoidance, which is entered when cwnd reaches the value of ssthresh. The congestion control strategies are shown in Figure 2.2.

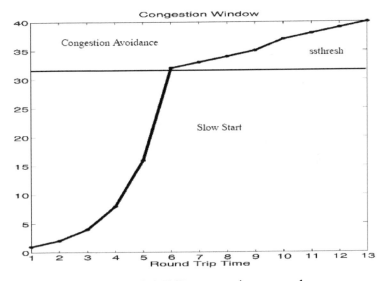

Fig. 2.2 TCP congestion control

In addition to the new congestion control strategy TCP Tahoe also proposes a new retransmission mechanism called Fast Retransmit. Fast Retransmit takes the reception of a threshold number of duplicate acknowledgments as loss indication and retransmits the packet immediately. A timeout is still used to recover losses; if not enough duplicate acknowledgments arrive. After a packet loss cwnd is set to 1 and Slow Start is re-entered. Ssthresh is set to half of the congestion window size when the loss occurred, which is considered as a safe transmission rate.

2.1.3 *TCP Reno*

TCP Reno adds one new mechanism called Fast Recovery to TCP Tahoe. Fast Recovery is only executed if a packet loss has been detected with Fast Retransmit. The reception of duplicate acknowledgments indicates that there are still some packets getting through the network, which is seen as a moderate congested state. In Fast Recovery cwnd, as well as ssthresh, are set to half of the congestion window size before the loss, then TCP Reno counts the incoming dupacks. Fast Recovery is ended when the first new acknowledgment arrives and Reno will directly enter Congestion Avoidance with half of the pre-loss congestion window.

2.1.4 *TCP NewReno*

TCP NewReno is the newest standardized TCP variant. It contains changes to both the congestion control and the retransmission mechanism of TCP Reno. TCP NewReno

10

extends Reno's Fast Recovery mechanism. When a packet loss is detected using Fast Retransmit, the highest sequence number transmitted so far is remembered, then Fast Recovery is entered. Fast Recovery is only ended when the acknowledgment for the highest sequence number sent before the loss is received. During a NewReno Fast Recovery additional losses are detected by the reception of partial acknowledgments. A partial acknowledgment is an acknowledgment for new data but with a lower sequence number than the highest data packet transmitted before the loss.

2.1.5 *Selective Acknowledgments (Sack)*

The use of Sacks permits the receiver to specify several additional data packets that have been received out-of-order within one dupack, instead of only the last in order packet received. This information enables the sender to retransmit lost packets faster than one packet per round trip time. Sack is a new retransmission strategy that theoretically could be used together with any congestion control mechanism.

2.1.6 *TCP Vegas*

TCP Vegas proposes its own unique retransmission and congestion control strategies. The main goal of its congestion control mechanism is to sense the beginning of congestion and to decrease its transmission rate before losses occur. To achieve this goal a measure for the congestion in the network is needed. TCP Vegas measures network congestion by comparing an expected throughput to the actual throughput of the connection. For the expected throughput a base round trip time is defined, which is the smallest round trip time that the connection has experienced during its lifetime. This is assumed to be the round trip time for the uncongested network.

2.1.7 *TCP Fack*

TCP Fack is Reno TCP with forward acknowledgment. For Fack the TCP performance is highest as expected. The design of Fack is same as the Reno and the forward acknowledgement is implemented. For wireless network where the loss probability is higher then the Fack will perform well.

2.2 TCP in Wireless or Cellular Mobile System

In recent years there has been a strong interest in extending the Internet access technologies to wireless (Cellular Mobile System links). There are many advantages in using these technologies. For example they enable user mobility and network access anytime from anywhere.

cwnd increase, it is obvious that the higher the round trip time the slower the congestion window growth. This is especially profound during the Slow Start phase which is meant to probe quickly for available bandwidth.

Long Time to Recover from Lost Packets: Since the loss detection is based on an exchange of acknowledgments it always takes at least one round trip time for the sender to detect the loss of one packet and to retransmit it. The retransmission timeout value is also based on the round trip time as well as the variation of the round trip time samples. Therefore the larger any one of these values is, the higher the retransmission timeout will be. A high timeout value means a potentially long idle time during which the connection waits for the timeout to expire and for data transmission to recommence. Finally, as already mentioned, each loss is taken as a congestion indication. After a loss the transmission rate is reduced.

Receive Window Limitation: For high delay (or high bandwidth) links this value is quite large and it is possible that TCP will never be able to use the available link bandwidth. This is caused by the receive window limitation. The advertised receive window is always the upper bound for the congestion window growth. Unfortunately there is only a 16 bit field in the TCP header reserved to transmit this receive window to the sender.

Variable Propagation Delay: Not too much research has been done up to date to investigate TCP behavior over networks with variable propagation delay.

2.3 TCP Header

Every TCP segment begins with a fixed-format, 20-byte header. The header fields are as follows:

> ➢ The SrcPort and DstPort fields identify the source and destination ports, respectively. These two fields plus the source and destination IP addresses, combine to uniquely identify each TCP connection.

> ➢ The sequence number identifies the byte in the stream of data from the sending TCP to the receiving TCP that the first byte of data in this segment represents.

> ➢ The Acknowledgement number field contains the next sequence number that the sender of the acknowledgement expects to receive. This is therefore the sequence number plus 1 of the last successfully received byte of data.

> ➢ The header length gives the length of the header in 32-bit words. This is required because the length of the options field is variable.

16

> ➢ The 6-bit Flags field is used to relay control information between TCP peers. The possible flags include SYN, FIN, RESET, PUSH, URG, and ACK [1].

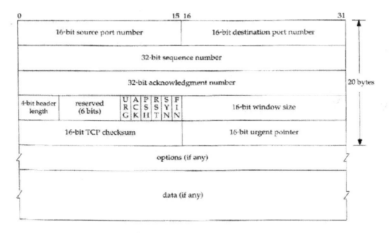

Fig. 2.3 TCP Header

- The SYN and Fin flags are used when establishing and terminating a TCP connection, respectively.

- The ACK flag is set any time the Acknowledgement field is valid, implying that the receiver should pay attention to it.

- The URG flag signifies that this segment contains urgent data. When this flag is set, the UrgPtr field indicates where the non-urgent data contained in this segment begins.

17

- The PUSH flag signifies that the sender invoked the push operation; which indicates to the receiving side of TCP that it should notify the receiving process of this fact.

- Finally, the RESET flag signifies that the receiver has become confused and so wants to abort the connection.

➢ The Checksum covers the TCP segment, the TCP header and the TCP data. This is a mandatory field that must be calculated by the sender, and then verified by the receiver.

➢ The Option field is the maximum segment size option, called the MSS. Each end of the connection normally specifies this option on the first segment exchanged. It specifies the maximum sized segment the sender wants to receive.

➢ The data portion of the TCP segment is optional.

2.4 TCP Transmission Policy

A simple transport protocol uses the following principle, send a packet and then wait for an acknowledgment from the receiver before sending the next packet. If the ACK is not received within a certain amount of time, retransmit the packet.

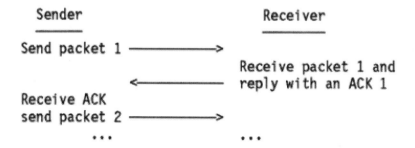

Fig. 2.4 Simple transmission-flows

While this mechanism ensures reliability, it only uses a part of the available network bandwidth.

2.4.1 The Window Principle

Consider now a protocol where the sender groups its packets to be transmitted as

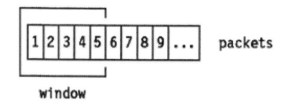

Fig. 2.5 Window principles and message packet

And use the following rules:

- The sender may send all packets within the window without receiving an ACK, but must start a timeout timer for each of them.

- The receiver must acknowledge each packet received, indicating the sequence number of the last well-received packet.

- The sender slides the window on each ACK received.

In our example, the sender may transmit packets 1 to 5 without waiting for any acknowledgment:

```
        Sender                      Network

        Send packet 1        ──────────>
        Send packet 2        ──────────>
        Send packet 3        ──────────>
        Send packet 4        ──────────>
ACK for packet 1 received  <──────────   ACK 1
        Send packet 5        ──────────>
```

Fig. 2.6 Window principles

At the moment the sender receives the ACK 1 (acknowledgment for packet 1), it may slide its window to exclude packet 1. At this point, the sender may also transmit packet 6.

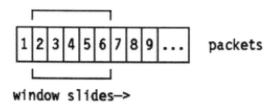

Fig. 2.7 Message packets

Imagine some special cases:

- Packet 2 gets lost: the sender will not receive an ACK 2, so its window will remain in the position 1 (as last picture above). In fact, as the receiver did not receive packet 2, it will acknowledge packets 3, 4 and 5 with an ACK 1, since packet 1 was the last one received ``in sequence". At the sender's side, eventually a timeout will occur for packet 2 and it will be retransmitted. Note that reception of this packet by the receiver will generate an ACK 5, since it has now successfully received all packets 1 to 5, and the sender's window will slide four positions upon receiving this ACK 5.

- Packet 2 did arrive, but the acknowledgment gets lost: the sender does not receive ACK 2, but will receive ACK 3. ACK 3 is an acknowledgment for all packets up to 3 (including packet 2) and the sender may now slide his window to packet 4.

This window mechanism ensures:

- Reliable transmission.

- Better use of the network bandwidth (better throughput).

- Flow-control, as the receiver may delay replying to a packet with an acknowledgment, knowing its free buffers available and the window-size of the communication.

The Window Principle Applied to TCP. The above window principle is used in TCP, but with a few differences:

- As TCP provides a byte-stream connection, sequence numbers are assigned to each byte in the stream. TCP divides this contiguous byte stream into TCP segments to transmit them. The window principle is used at the byte level; that is, the segments sent and ACKs received will carry byte-sequence numbers and the window size is expressed as a number of bytes, rather than a number of packets.

- The receiver determines the window size, when the connection is established, and is variable during the data transfer. Each ACK message will include the window-size that the receiver is ready to deal with at that particular time.

The sender's data stream can now be seen as:

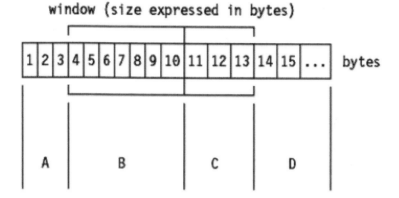

Fig. 2.8 Window principles applied to TCP

Where:

A- Bytes that are transmitted and have been acknowledged.

B- Bytes that are sent but not yet acknowledged.

C- Bytes that may be sent without waiting for any acknowledgment.

D- Bytes that may not yet be sent.

Ensure that TCP will block bytes into segments, and a TCP segment only carries the sequence number of the first byte in the segment.

2.4.2 *Acknowledgments and Retransmissions*

TCP sends data in variable length segments. Sequence numbers are based on a byte count. Acknowledgments specify the sequence number of the next byte that the receiver expects to receive.

Now suppose that a segment gets lost or corrupted. In this case, the receiver will acknowledge all further well-received segments with an acknowledgment referring to the first byte of the missing packet. The sender will stop transmitting when it has sent all the bytes in the window. Eventually, a timeout will occur and the missing segment will be retransmitted.

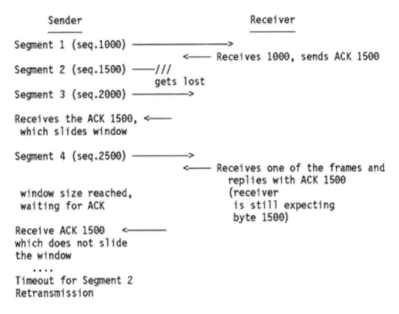

```
        Sender                              Receiver
        _____                              _____
Segment 1 (seq.1000) ------------------->
                              <------ Receives 1000, sends ACK 1500
Segment 2 (seq.1500) ------///
                        gets lost
Segment 3 (seq.2000) ------------->

Receives the ACK 1500, <------
which slides window

Segment 4 (seq.2500) ------------->
                              <------ Receives one of the frames and
                                     replies with ACK 1500
        window size reached,         (receiver
        waiting for ACK              is still expecting
                                     byte 1500)
Receive ACK 1500   <------
which does not slide
the window
    ....
Timeout for Segment 2
Retransmission
```

Fig. 2.9 Acknowledgment and retransmission process

Suppose a window size of 1500 bytes, and segments of 500 bytes. A problem now arises, since the sender does know that segment 2 is lost or corrupted, but doesn't know anything about segments 3 and 4. The sender should at least retransmit segment 2, but it could also retransmit segments 3 and 4 (since they are within the current window).

1. Segment 3 has been received, and for segment 4 it is not known: it could be received, but ACK didn't reach us yet, or it could be lost also.

2. Segment 3 was lost, and received the ACK 1500 upon the reception of segment 4.

2.5 Error Control

Error control is a necessary function in communication networks. In general, several different error-handling mechanisms co-exist in the same network. Some errors are caused by short-lived noise in a specific location of the network that causes individual bits in the data stream to be altered. This is a problem of the physical transmission of information, for example thermal noise in the electronic components can cause errors. These types of errors are called bit errors, noise-induced errors or transmission errors. A second type of error occurs on a higher layer in the network, where packets are switched

25

through different links. If links are overloaded, packets May have to be dropped due to limited buffer space in the routers or switches, this is known as congestion losses. There are two main approaches for handling errors and losses,

- o Retransmission &

- o Forward Error Correction (FEC).

2.5.1 *Retransmission*

When retransmissions are used, all packets in which errors are detected are discarded. Hence, losses are caused by packets being discarded either due to transmission errors or due to congestion. Packets that have been discarded must be retransmitted by means of automatic repeat request (ARQ) protocols.

The retransmission of lost data can also be handled in different ways, one approach is that the acknowledgements specify exactly the missing packets, and only those packets are retransmitted, which is known as selective repeat.

2.5.2 *Forward Error Correction*

The second approach to handling errors and losses is forward error correction, where redundant information is proactively sent to the receiver in order to allow it to correct errors. The redundant information is generated by means of channel coding.

Channel coding is used in many commercial systems, for example compact discs and mobile communication systems. There are several types of channel codes, and the ones used in this thesis are block codes. In this section alternative codes are shortly described.

2.5.2.1 *Block Codes*

A block code is applied to a block of data symbols and generates a number of redundant symbols, also called. parity symbols. Each symbol consists of one or more bits, depending on the code. The error correction capability is higher for codes with more parity symbols, but the parity symbols also use some of the transmission capacity. Well-known examples of block codes are Hamming codes, Reed-Solomon codes and Bose – Chaudhuri – Hochquenghem (BCH) codes.

Last code word of block ↓

Packet 1	First data symbol code word →	
Packet 2		
Packet N-1		
Packet N		
Redundancy packet 1	Redundancy symbol →	
Redundancy packet 2		

Fig. 2.10 Block coding technique

27

To correct bit errors a block of bits is encoded and transmitted over a link, then the decoder attempts to correct bit errors if any are present. If the number of bit errors within a block is lower than the code can correct, the original data block is recovered.

In packet loss recovery a block of packets is encoded to generate packets of parity information, i.e. the first symbols in each data packet are encoded to produce the first symbols in each of the parity packets as shown in Figure 2.10 .

2.5.2.2 Fountain Codes

The decoding complexity of block codes in general increases rapidly with the code length. Recent progress in the area of channel codes has lead to the development of codes with decoding complexity that only grows linearly with the code length. These are actually a form of low-density parity check codes that were initially proposed by Gallagher in 1963, but practical codes have only been developed in the 1990's. For the erasure channel these codes are known as fountain codes due to their application in the digital fountain concept for distribution of large files.

2.5.2.3 *Convolution Codes*

The encoding is performed by a digital finite impulse response (FIR) filter. The data does not have to be divided into blocks before the encoding, as opposed to block codes. The decoding is usually made by the Viterbi algorithm, where the states of the encoding filter are represented by different nodes in a trellis, and the transitions between different states are represented as edges.

2.5.2.4 *Turbo Codes*

Turbo codes are based on combining several encoders using interleaving to produce codes of very long lengths with limited decoding complexity. The basic codes of the turbo codes can either be block codes or convolutional codes. Decoding is made by means of message passing between multiple decoders, similarly to the decoding of low-density parity check codes. For end-to-end FEC it does not have any clear advantages.

3

TCP in NS-2 and Simulation of Experiment

This section describes the operation of the TCP agents in ns. There are two major types of TCP agents: one-way agents and a two-way agent. One-way agents are further subdivided into a set of TCP senders (which obey different congestion and error control techniques) and receivers ("sinks"). The two-way agent is symmetric in the sense that it represents both a sender and receiver. It is still under development.

3.1 Supported Senders and Receivers

The one-way TCP sending agents currently supported are:

Agent/TCP - a "tahoe" TCP sender

Agent/TCP/Reno - a "Reno" TCP sender

Agent/TCP/NewReno - Reno with a modification

Agent/TCP/Sack1 - TCP with selective repeat

Agent/TCP/Vegas - TCP Vegas

Agent/TCP/Fack - Reno TCP with "forward acknowledgment"

The one-way TCP receiving agents currently supported are:

Agent/TCPSink - TCP sink with one ACK per packet

Agent/TCPSink/DelAck - TCP sink with configurable delay per ACK

Agent/TCPSink/Sack1 - selective ACK sink

Agent/TCPSink/Sack1/DelAck - Sack1 with DelAck

The simulator supports several versions of an abstracted TCP sender. These objects attempt to capture the essence of the TCP congestion and error control behaviors, but are not intended to be faithful replicas of real-world TCP implementations.

3.2 TCP Routing Agent

There are several approaches in conventional routing algorithm in traditional wire line networks, and some ideas from these are also used in ad-hoc networks. Among the traditional approaches the followings are used generally:

- ➤ Link State

- ➤ Destination Sequenced Distance Vector -DSDV

- ➤ Dynamic Source routing -DSR

- ➤ Flooding

3.2.1 *Destination Sequenced Distance Vector-DSDV*

DSDV is a distance vector routing protocol. Each node has a routing table that indicates for each destination, which is the next hop and number of hops to the destination. Each node periodically broadcast routing updates. A sequence no is used to tag each route. It shows the freshness of the route: a route with higher sequence no is more favorable. In addition among two routed with the same sequence no, the one with less hops is more favorable. If a node detects that a route to a destination has broken, then its hop no is set to infinity and its sequence no updated but assigned an odd number: even numbers corresponds to sequence numbers of connected paths.

3.2.2 *Ad-hoc On Demand Distance Vector – AODV*

AODV is a distance vector type routing. It does not require nodes to maintain routes to destination that are not actively used. As long as the endpoints of a communication connection have valid routes to each other, AODV does not play a role. The protocol uses different messages to discover and maintain links: Route Requests (RREQ), Route Replies (RREPs), and Route Errors (RERRs). These message types are received via UDP, and normal IP header processing applies. AODV does not allow to handle unidirectional links.

3.2.3 *Dynamic Source Routing – DSR*

Designed for mobile ad hoc networks with up to around two hundred nodes with possibly high mobility rate. The protocol works "on demand", i.e. without any periodic updates. Packets carry along the complete path they should take. This reduces overheads for large routing updates at the network. The nodes store in their cache all known routes. The protocol is composed of route discovery and route maintenance.

It consists of the following two steps

> ➤ Route discovery

> ➤ Route maintenance

3.2.4 *Temporally Ordered Routing Algorithm-TORA*

This protocol is of the family of link reversal protocols. It may provide several routes between a source and a destination. TORA contains three parts: creating, maintaining and erasing routes. At each node, a separate copy of TORA is run per each destination. TORA builds a directed acyclic graph rooted at the destination. It associated a height with each node in the network. Messages flow from nodes with higher height to those with lower heights. Routes are discovered using Query and Update packets.

33

3.3 Simulation Topology

In real world, number of senders and receivers as well as their relative position, internal communication can be various in patterns. Different types of protocols can also be used in the same network. Such type of network has been considered for our experiment. TCP and UDP protocols are have been taken hare under consideration and link between two routers are duplex. Duplex channel is necessary due to the presence of TCP sender because acknowledgement of each received packet must be propagated through this channel in reverse order from destination to source.

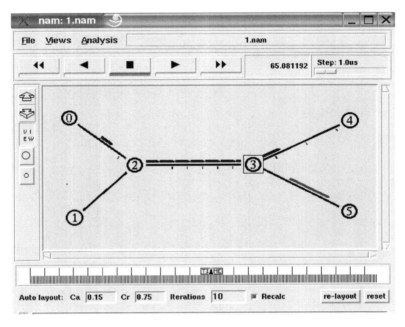

Fig. 3.1 Simulation topology

Although UDP sender has been used, calculations were performed for TCP. Bandwidth and propagation delay of this channel highly affect the transmission of packets. TCP performance has been measured with respect to these parameter variations effectively.

3.4 Network Implementation

Initially propagation delay for all the links has been chosen 10ms, effective bandwidth 100Mb and buffer management technology were DropTail. Packet sending rate for two senders were 1.0Mbps but they were varied during performance analysis.

3.5 TCP Connection Establishment

At the starting, by transmitting the packets named SYNC and ACK (of 40 bytes each) between source and destination, TCP connection establishment is accomplished as shown in Figure 3.2.

```
+  1 0 2 tcp 40 - - - - - - - - 1 0.0 4.0 0 2
-  1 0 2 tcp 40 - - - - - - - - 1 0.0 4.0 0 2
r  1.01004 0 2 tcp 40 - - - - - - - 1 0.0 4.0
+  1.01004 2 3 tcp 40 - - - - - - - 1 0.0 4.0
-  1.01004 2 3 tcp 40 - - - - - - - 1 0.0 4.0
r  1.02036 2 3 tcp 40 - - - - - - - 1 0.0 4.0
+  1.02036 3 4 tcp 40 - - - - - - - 1 0.0 4.0
-  1.02036 3 4 tcp 40 - - - - - - - 1 0.0 4.0
r  1.050424 3 4 tcp 40 - - - - - - - 1 0.0 4.0
+  1.150424 4 3 ack 40 - - - - - - - 1 4.0 0.0
-  1.150424 4 3 ack 40 - - - - - - - 1 4.0 0.0
r  1.180488 4 3 ack 40 - - - - - - - 1 4.0 0.0
+  1.180488 3 2 ack 40 - - - - - - - 1 4.0 0.0
-  1.180488 3 2 ack 40 - - - - - - - 1 4.0 0.0
r  1.190808 3 2 ack 40 - - - - - - - 1 4.0 0.0
+  1.190808 2 0 ack 40 - - - - - - - 1 4.0 0.0
-  1.190808 2 0 ack 40 - - - - - - - 1 4.0 0.0
r  1.200848 2 0 ack 40 - - - - - - - 1 4.0 0.0
```

Fig. 3.2 Segment of trace file showing TCP connection establishment

3.6 Running the Simulation Program

In the OTcl script, the program "1.tcl" was written to implement the network for simulation. To run it, command line *ns 1.tcl* is enough in the shell.

FTP sessions had been created between a TCP source and a TCP sink. Data transfer between source and sink will be performed via a base station, source is connected to base station through full duplex wired link and sink is connected to base station via wireless link. The TCP throughput at sink will be calculated. This TCP throughput is the performance parameter. TCP Throughput for various TCP Source and Sinks for various throughput vs time, congestion window vs time and for throughput vs various delay of the wired link are mentioned here.

3.7 Structure of Trace File

Trace file consist of all the information of simulation. To analyze the simulation trace file information is extracted from the trace file using a program. The information is easily distinguished able because they maintain a order between them. Each column (from left to right) of trace file contains data about the following parameters.

E v e n t	T i m e	From node	To node	Pkt type	Pkt size	F l a g s	F i d	S r c a d d r	D s t a d d r	S e q n u m	P k t i d

Fig. 3.3 Fields appearing in a trace file

Functions with their brief description have been provided as below:

37

TABLE 3.1 Trace file data explanation

Field position	Function of the field
1	Operation performed in the simulation
2	Simulation time of event occurrence
3	Node 1 of what is being traced
4	Node 2 of what is being traced
5	Packet type
6	Packet size
7	Flags
8	IP flow identifier
9	Packet source node address
10	Packet destination node address
11	Sequence number
12	Unique packet identifier

i.   The first field is the event type. It is given by four possible symbols r,+,-,d which corresponds respectively to receive, enqueued, dequeued and dropped.

ii. The second field indicates the time of event occurs.

iii.   Gives the input node of the link at which the event occurs.

iv.   Gives the output node of the link at which the event occurs.

v.   Gives the packet type. It may be TCP, CBR , ACK so on. It depends on the applications.

vi.   Gives the packet size.

vii.   Some flags.

viii.   This is the flow id(fid) of IPv6 that the user can set for each flow at the input OTcl script. This field can be used for further analysis. This field is used to specify the color of the NAM display.

ix.   It is the source address given in the form 'node.port'.

x.   It is the destination address given in the same form of source address.

xi.   This is the network layer protocol's packet sequence number. Even through UDP implementations in a real network do not use sequence number, ns keeps track of UDP packet sequence number for analysis purposes.

xii.   The last field shows the unique id of the packet.

3.8 Calculating the Throughput

To find the throughput a Perl code tput.perl has been used. It calculates the throughput for various times separately. For this thesis total 120s simulation is considered. So this tput.perl will find the throughput for 0s, 10s, 20s, 30s, 40s, 50s, 60s, 70s, 80s, 90s, 100s, 110s, and 120s. This throughput is calculated using the trace file created by the simulation program. This file contains all the information about the simulation program. This throughput program stored the separate throughput for all the separate time in to another file. This file is used for drawing graph using gnuPlot. The code for calculating the throughput has been given in appendix A.

3.9 Forward Error Correction Using gnuC++

Forward error correction depends on the sender end and receiver end.

3.9.1 *Designing the Sender*

Steps of sender design

➢ Read the content of packet in binary format from a file

➢ Construct the packet header

➢ Generate the checksum

➢ Send the packet to the receiver

➢ Start the timer to check the time out

➢ Update the window size

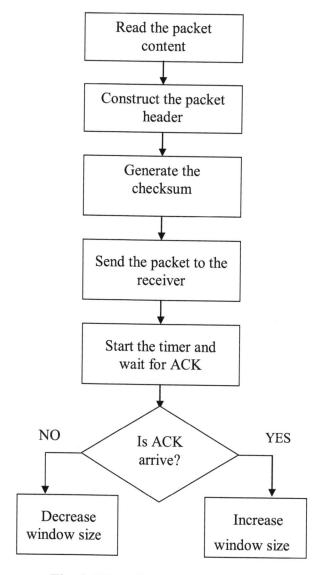

Fig. 3.4 Flowchart at the sender end

3.9.2 *Designing the Receiver*

Steps of receiver design

➢ Receive the packet

➢ Generate the checksum and compare with the existing checksum

➢ If any error is found then try to correct error

➢ If error correction is possible or no error occurs then send ack packet

➢ If error correction is not possible discard the packet and wait for a retransmitted packet.

Here one sender and one receiver is used. The link between the sender and the receiver is wired and bidirectional. The link is used for packet and acknowledgement transmission between the sender and the receiver.

3.9.3 *Parameters of FEC*

The following parameters are varied for Forward Error Correction (FEC):-

➢ Congestion Window

➢ Time out

➢ Retransmission if error correction is not possible

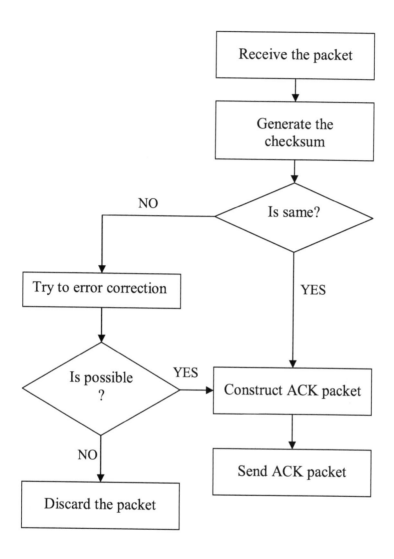

Fig. 3.5 Flowchart of processing at the receiver end

4

Experimental Results

To analyze the performance among various TCP senders and receivers five parameters have been used. They are:

- Packet Vs Bandwidth

- Packet Vs Propagation Delay

- Packet Vs Rate

- Buffer Volume vs Time

- Bss vs Time

4.1 Packet Vs Bandwidth

We varied the bandwidth each time and the number of packets was counted at destination node 2 during entire simulation period from trace file whose amount was as in Table 4.1. As bandwidth of channel increases, number of packet received also increases by different magnitude for different variants. Highest number of packet is obtained for NewRenoASYM (NewReno in the asymmetry channel). But TCP Tahoe, Reno, NewReno, Sack1 and Vegas behave identically with bandwidth variation of the channel which generates common curve in the Figure 4.1.

44

TABLE 4.1 Packet received at different bandwidth

TCP variants	Packets at Bandwidth			
	2 Mb	8 Mb	16 Mb	32 Mb
Tahoe	3214	3270	3280	3310
Reno	3214	3270	3280	3310
NewReno	3214	3270	3280	3310
NewRenoASYM	3247	3305	3317	3347
sack1	3214	3270	3280	3310
Vegas	3214	3270	3280	3310
Fack	3127	3191	3203	3233

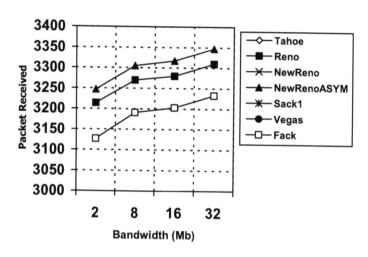

Fig. 4.1 Packet vs. bandwidth

4.2 Packet Vs Delay

We performed packet count for several propagation delays in the code line mentioned above incase of all TCP variants whose nature was as in Figure 4.2.

45

TABLE 4.2 Packet received at different propagation delay

TCP variants	Packets at Delay				
	10 ms	20 ms	30 ms	40 ms	50 ms
Tahoe	6869	6479	6215	5973	5673
Reno	6869	6479	6215	5973	5673
NewReno	6869	6479	6215	5973	5673
NewrenoASYM	6869	6479	6215	5973	5673
sack1	6869	6479	6215	5973	5673
Vegas	7200	6812	6400	6091	5934
Fack	6869	6479	6215	5973	5673

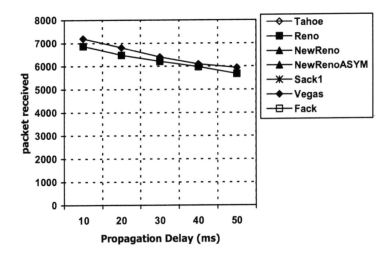

Fig. 4.2 Packet vs. propagation delay.

Although amount of packet received is inversely proportional to propagation delay, 'Vegas' has the best performance due to its improved retransmission technique.

4.3 Packet Vs Rate

The nature of TCPs to packet sending rate consists of basically two phases (refer Figure 4.3):

1) **Linearly Increasing Phase:** Each TCP agent (sender) increases the packet estimation to be sent after getting the acknowledgement of previously sent packets. The slope of curve at any point within this region is bounded by the domain (0, 1).

2) **Saturation Phase:** TCP reaches in this phase when each agent consume their maximum allowable channel proportion which is also called **DC** state having constant slope equivalent to *zero*.

In this case, Newreno, NewrenoASYM, Sack1 and Fack show the best performance as they increase congestion window size exponentially with rate provided that no congestion occurred in the channel.

TABLE 4.3 Packet received at different rate

TCP variants	Packets at Rate			
	5 Mbps	10 Mbps	15 Mbps	20 Mbps
Tahoe	16110	33388	33625	33507
Reno	16110	33388	33625	33507
Newreno	20372	34928	34809	34928
NewrenoASYM	20372	34928	34809	34928
Sack1	20372	34928	34809	34928
Vegas	14131	33009	33009	33009
Fack	20372	34928	34809	34928

Nature of packet variation becomes-

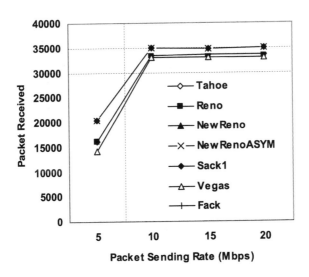

Fig. 4.3 Packet vs. transmission rate

4.4 Buffer Volume Vs Time

Internally buffer volume posses a close connection with 'bandwidth delay product' which is defined by-

$$bw \_ del \_ prod \ (packets \ ) = \frac{bw \ (bits \ / \sec) \ * \ RTT \ (\sec)}{8 \ * \ MSS \ (bytes \ )}$$

TCP can only achieve its optimal throughput if the minimal buffer size on the path is equal to the bandwidth delay product. If the minimal buffer size is larger, a constant backlog of packets builds up in the buffer wasting network resources and introducing latency. If it is smaller, the congestion window will

48

never be able to reach the necessary size to utilize the available bandwidth. If the buffer size is larger than the bandwidth during *Slow Start*, the congestion window needs to be able to reach $2*(bw\_del\_prod + buffer\_size)$ to achieve optimal throughput. The receiver's advertised window, which is always an upper bound to the congestion window, has to be set to a large enough value for this growth. Window scaling might be necessary to achieve this.

During Congestion Avoidance we have

$$\text{max\_} cwnd = bw\_del\_prod + buffer\_size \quad \text{and}$$

$$ssthresh = \frac{bw\_del\_prod + buffer\_size}{2}.$$

This equals to

$$ssthresh = bw\_del\_prod + \frac{(buffer\_size - bw\_del\_prod)}{2}$$

.

Case 1:

If the buffer size is larger than the bandwidth delay product the term $\dfrac{(buffer\_size - bw\_del\_prod)}{2}$ is greater than zero and equal to the amount of packets that always remain in the buffer and cause constant congestion.

Case 2:

On the other hand if $\dfrac{(buffer\_size - bw\_del\_prod)}{2}$ is

negative, *ssthresh* will always be remaining below the bandwidth delay product and the connection will never be able to achieve optimal throughput. In this case $\dfrac{(buffer\_size - bw\_del\_prod)}{2}$ indicates the number of

packets that should have been in the buffer to avoid link idle time.

4.4.1 *Algorithm to Calculate Buffer Size*

Input: {*time, Bcs, Tcs, Ts, cwnd_*}.

> *Bcs*: current size of *buffer*.

> *Ts* and *Tcs*: total and current simulation time.

> *cwnd_*: variable of *Agent Class*.

Output: {*OFILE*: o/p file holding *time* and *buffer*}.

1. set *time*: =0.1
2. set *Bcs*: =current value of *cwnd_*
3. save in *OFILE* = [*time, Bcs*]
4. set *time*: = *time* + *Tcs*
5. iff *time*<*Ts* then goto step 2
6. Plot *OFILE* and EXIT.

Here, *cwnd_* refers the congestion window volume. Congestion window is defined as the number of packet that a source can transmit after getting the acknowledgment of previously sent packets. This window size varies depending on a range of network parameters.

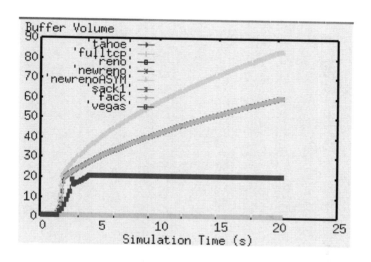

Fig. 4.4 Graph of buffer volume vs. time

Active buffer volume dynamically changes, shown by the curve family in figure 4.4. FullTcp shows nearly zero level buffer utilization, Tahoe and Vegas have identical shape with much improved utilization than FullTcp. Again, Sack1 and Fack maintain analogous improved policy of buffer allocation than the previous variants. It is evident from the figure 4.4 that buffer utilization by NewRenoASYM is optimal.

4.5 Bss Vs Time

Bss (Successfully Sent Byte) is calculated directly from the trace file by applying a set of checking and summation operation as depicted in the flowchart of Figure 4.6. Each row of the trace file has been taken into array where symbols of the row are stored as array index on which several conditional checking are applied to extract the exact data required to find Bss.

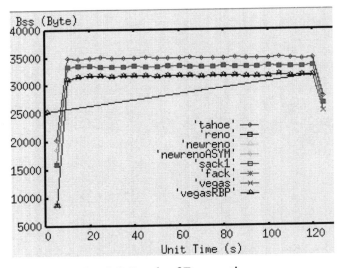

Fig. 4.5 Graph of Bss vs. time

Reno, Vegas and VegasRBP show the poorest performance under this criterion but NewReno, Fack and Sack1 have comparatively improved performance. Tahoe is the best performer for successfully Byte sending as implied in Figure 4.5.

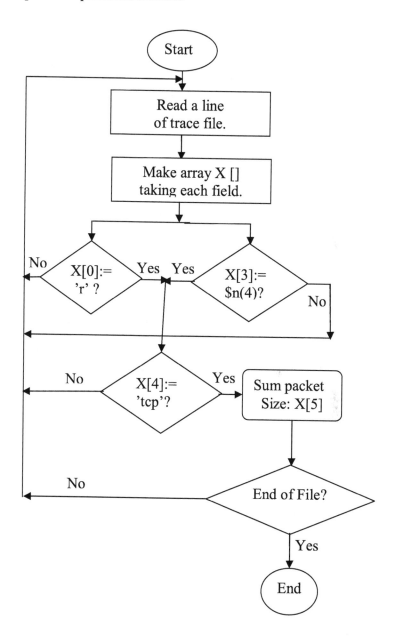

Fig. 4.6 Flowchart to calculate Bss

4.6 TCP Performance Improvement

In general TCP, packet transmission follows buffered model in which separate buffers are enacted for sender and receiver [6, 8] that accept packets according to queue order. Our proposed architecture includes a bypass mechanism which acts as error detection and correction scheme at Data Link layer of transmission. Incase of TCP, for each packet (fair or corrupted) reached in receiver, acknowledgement is sent to the sender [8]. So basic traveling period spent for an i-th packet is given by $2*\partial_i$, where ∂_i is one way quantum needed for i-th packet or acknowledgement to travel from source to destination or vice-versa.

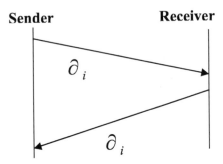

Fig. 4.7 Packet and acknowledgement transmission

The principle of TCP is to retransmit a packet several times if it is not successfully reached to receiver. This *retransmission technique* is ineffective incase of erroneous unfair wireless channel where packet will be always corrupted before reaching destination and $2*\partial_i$ time will be spent ideally. To get ride of this situation we have proposed the model that yields desired solution as our Network Simulator (NS-2) simulation depicts.

4.6.1 *Mathematical Basis of Proposed Model*

Consider N_{pd} is number of corrupted packets, $t_r(N_{pd})$ and $t_c(N_{pd})$ indicates retransmission time and correction time of N_{pd} packets respectively. T_{save} is saved time, obtained by correcting the packets in place of retransmission. Thus it provides much time interval within which more and more packets are sent. N_{AFEC} refers the number of packets that can be successfully sent in our Adaptive Forward Error Correction (AFEC) model and N_{GTCP} refers the packets for general TCP with traditional model.

$$t_r(N_{pd}) > t_c(N_{pd})$$

$$t_r(N_{pd}) = 2 * \sum_{i=1}^{N_{pd}} \partial_i$$

$$t_c(N_{pd}) = N_{pd} * T_c$$

$$T_{save} = t_r(N_{pd}) - t_c(N_{pd})$$

$$T_{NEW} = T_{OLD} + T_{save}$$

$$N_{AFEC} = N_{T_{NEW}}$$

$$\because T_{NEW} > T_{OLD}$$

$$\therefore N_{AFEC} > N_{GTCP}$$

Aforementioned mathematical relationship shows that our proposed architecture provides more packets than that of traditional model within same duration which proves its effectiveness.

Subsequent experimental results express that TCP performance will be improved regarding to other perspectives as well using this model.

4.6.2 *Coding Information*

Many error detection and correction codes such as Hamming code, Reed Solomon (RS) code, CRC e.t.c are in existence but we have preferred Hamming code for its lower order complexity ($O(n)$ for n bit packet) whose principle would be shortly mentioned later. We have implemented this versatile Hamming code by TCL (Tool Command Language) and some portion by gnuC++ to verify our thinking in Network Simulator 2.

4.7 Policy of Hamming Code

The function H (m+r, m) indicates that if original data block has 'm' bits, it is enlarged to 'm+r' by adding 'r' redundant checksum bits where 'r' is calculated from the following inequality:

$$2^r \geq m + r + 1.$$

4.7.1 *Position of Redundant Bits*

Position of the checksum bits ($R_1, R_2, ...R_r$) in the packet are determined by

$R_{i+1}=2^i$ where i=0, 1, 2 ....(r-1). For 7 bits data bock it needs 4 check sum bits whose position will be as below:

Data:	D_7	D_6	D_5	D_4	D_3	D_2	D_1

Hamming Code:

H_{11}	H_{10}	H_9	H_8	H_7	H_6	H_5	H_4	H_3	H_2	H_1
D_7	D_6	D_5	R_4	D_4	D_3	D_2	R_3	D_1	R_2	R_1

4.7.2 *Values of Redundant Bits*

We have to consider all the 'r' bit binary numbers from '1' to 'm+r' (here 1 to 11 for 4 redundant bits) shown in table 4.4. For each binary sub column from LSB to MSB, we have to consider the cell containing '1'. Then the corresponding decimal numbers indicate the original data bit numbers on which X-OR (exclusive OR) operation has to be performed to get 'R' values.

57

TABLE 4.4 Bit selection table to find the '*R*' values

DECIMAL	BINARY			
1	0	0	0	1
2	0	0	1	0
3	0	0	1	1
4	0	1	0	0
5	0	1	0	1
6	0	1	1	0
7	0	1	1	1
8	1	0	0	0
9	1	0	0	1
10	1	0	1	0
11	1	0	1	1

Thus we get:

$$R_1 = H_3 \oplus H_5 \oplus H_7 \oplus H_9 \oplus H_{11}$$

$$R_2 = H_3 \oplus H_6 \oplus H_7 \oplus H_{10} \oplus H_{11}$$

$$R_3 = H_5 \oplus H_6 \oplus H_7$$

$R_4 = H_9 \oplus H_{10} \oplus H_{11}$, where any H_i indicates i th bit of hamming code.

4.7.3 *Error Detection*

At the receiver end, all the check bits

$$C_1 = H_1 \oplus H_3 \oplus H_5 \oplus H_7 \oplus H_9 \oplus H_{11}$$

$$C_2 = H_2 \oplus H_3 \oplus H_6 \oplus H_7 \oplus H_{10} \oplus H_{11}$$

$$C_3 = H_4 \oplus H_5 \oplus H_6 \oplus H_7$$

$$C_4 = H_8 \oplus H_9 \oplus H_{10} \oplus H_{11}$$

Are re-calculated. If (C_4 C_3 C_2 C_1) represent 'ZERO' then no error occurred, otherwise error occurred and the non-zero value indicates corrupted bit position in the received packet.

4.7.4 *Error Correction*

Simply perform negation ('NOT') operation on the value of corrupted bit position. That is if D_{OLD} be corrupted bit then after error correction we will get $D_{NEW} = \overline{D_{OLD}}$.

4.8 Overall Observation

Three important outcomes have been obtained from the experiment: A *decision table* for selecting the best TCP in a certain platform, Improvement of the *number of received packets*, Improvement of *buffer utilization*.

4.8.1 *Selecting the Best TCP*

A sharp analysis of the above data tables and curves connotes the decision table below:

TABLE 4.5 The best TCP selection table.

PARAMETERS	THE BEST TCP
Packet Vs Bandwidth	NewRenoASYM
Packet Vs Delay	Vegas
Packet Vs Rate	Sack1,Fack,NewRenoASYM
Buffer Vs Time	NewRenoASYM
Bss Vs Time interval	Tahoe

4.8.2 *Packet Vs Time*

During a certain simulation time, the number of received packets at receiver node was higher for proposed TCP than the original TCP. In noisy channel if any packet became corrupted, TCP retransmit its fresh copy several times which unfruitfully consume more CPU cycles, channel bandwidth and other resources. Everything can de reduced by packet correction at destination because corrected packet does not need re-transmission, as a result we can obtain relatively more and more data within same time interval as shown in the table 4.6 and figure 4.8.

TABLE 4.6 Packets for 'Traditional' and 'Proposed' TCP

Simulation Time (Sec)	Packet received for	
	Traditional TCP	Proposed TCP
0	0	0
5	403	450
10	813	903
20	1611	1789
30	2416	2684
40	3268	3631
50	4035	4483
60	4909	5454

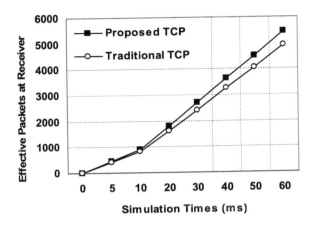

Fig. 4.8 Graph of packet vs. time

4.8.3 *Buffer Utilization*

T_s and A_s refers Total size (predefined) and Active buffer size. Corrupted packets are never included in the buffer so a large volume of buffer remains idle for general TCP, which indicates poor resource utilization. But their instantaneous correction solves the incident wisely. Proportion of idle buffer we have obtained from the equation below.

$$Percentage \_ of \_ Idle \_ buffer = \frac{(T_s - A_s)}{T_s} * 100 \%$$

TABLE 4.7 Idle buffer for 'Traditional' and 'Proposed' TCP

Simulation time (Sec)	Proportion of buffer remains idle (Receiver)	
	Traditional TCP	Proposed TCP
0	100%	100%
5	93.28%	92.41%
10	86.45%	84.95%
20	73.15%	70.18%
30	59.73%	55.26%
40	45.53%	39.48%
50	32.75%	25.28%
60	18.18%	9.10%

As time passes, active size of buffer begins to increase thus percentage of idle buffer decreases. Corrupted packets are never included into buffer, so a large portion of it remains idle for noisy channel as found in the above data table incase of 'General TCP'. But instantaneous correction of packets (which is our target) at this point can fruitfully improve such undeserving behavior of wireless TCP. Incase of 'Proposed TCP', the proportion of idle buffer is much less than that of 'General TCP' which implies higher degree buffer utilization. The proposed model is able to improve wireless TCP performance in unfair situation even when probability of packet loss becomes nearly 100%.

5

Literature Review

5.1 Discussion

Fall and Floyd evaluated the performance of TCP Reno, New Reno and SACK by simulations that focused on comparing the differences of packet loss recovery mechanisms [14]. In addition, in their simulation, packet loss occurrence was designed specifically to highlight the improved performance of SACK. Lakshman and Madhow investigated the performance of TCP Tahoe and Reno in the presence of large bandwidth-delay product and random losses [15]. They assumed finite buffer size. Nayma and Sumyea analysis of TCP Tahoe, Reno and New Reno and Sack over cellular mobile system but they do not consider Vegas and Fack, they consider two parameters (bit error rate, hand off) for performance analysis [1] and do not vary TCP receivers. But in this thesis investigation is done for six TCP senders and four TCP receivers, here three parameters are used to compare between them and the effect of forward error correction is also shown over wireless noisy channel.

Forward error correction is also used to increase the throughput for wireless link in the simulating environment of gnuC++. To improve the performance of TCP, hamming code has been implemented. Simulation results show some important characteristics for TCP senders and receivers for wireless link and also show some positive effects of using AFEC on the TCP throughput in a simple mixed (wired-cum–wireless) network. The performance should behave same for various network and load situations.

5.2 Further Study

At first the comparison among various TCP versions for five parameters   have been implemented. But observing TCP performance with respect other networking criteria can be a future task. Secondly, Hamming code has been used for adaptive forward error correction but hamming code can only recover single bit error. Multiple bits error can also be handled with a little degree limitations by executing several nested loopings. But this needs *splitting and merging* operations and can serve as multiple bits solution for a *Packet, not a frame.* That is why other forward error correction algorithm (for an example Reed Solomon Code) can also be implemented and their relative performance can be evaluated. Wireless channel standard Orinoco 802.11b 11Mbps pc card has been used in our thesis work. For more simulation should other standards can be considered.

Appendix

Appendix A

```
set ns [new Simulator]
$ns color 1 blue
$ns color 2 Red
set tf [open 1.tr w]
set winfile [open WinFile w]
$ns trace-all $tf
set nf [open 1.nam w]
$ns namtrace-all $nf

proc finish { } {
global ns tf nf
$ns flush-trace
close $tf
close $nf
exec nam 1.nam &
exit 0
}
#Create six nodes
set n0 [$ns node]
set n1 [$ns node]
set n2 [$ns node]
set n3 [$ns node]
set n4 [$ns node]
set n5 [$ns node]

$ns duplex-link $n0 $n2 2Mb 10ms DropTail
$ns duplex-link $n1 $n2 2Mb 10ms DropTail
$ns duplex-link $n2 $n3 0.3Mb 100ms DropTail
$ns duplex-link $n3 $n4 0.5Mb 40ms DropTail
$ns duplex-link $n3 $n5 0.5Mb 30ms DropTail

set tcp [new Agent/TCP]
#set tcp [new Agent/TCP/FullTcp]
#set tcp [new Agent/TCP/Reno]
#set tcp [new Agent/TCP/Newreno]
#set tcp [new Agent/TCP/Newreno/Asym]
```

Appendix

```
#set tcp [new Agent/TCP/Sack1]
#set tcp [new Agent/TCP/Vegas]
#set tcp [new Agent/TCP/Fack]

set sink [new Agent/TCPSink]
#set sink [new Agent/TCPSink/DelAck]
#set sink [new Agent/TCPSink/Sack1]
#set sink [new Agent/TCPSink/Sack1/DelAck]

$ns attach-agent $n0 $tcp
$ns attach-agent $n4 $sink
$ns connect $tcp $sink
$tcp set fid_ 1
$tcp set packetSize_ 552

set ftp [new Application/FTP]
$ftp attach-agent $tcp

set udp [new Agent/UDP]
$ns attach-agent $n1 $udp
set null  [new Agent/Null]
$ns attach-agent $n5 $null
$ns connect $udp $null
$udp set fid_ 2

set cbr [new Application/Traffic/CBR]
$cbr attach-agent $udp
$cbr set packetSize_ 1000
$cbr set rate_ 0.01Mb

$ns at 0.1 "$cbr start"
$ns at 1.0 "$ftp start"
$ns at 124.0 "$ftp stop"
$ns at 124.5 "$cbr stop"

$ns at 125.0 "finish"
$ns run
```

****

Appendix B

***** Forward error correction using gnuC++****

//Sender input generation

```
#include<fstream.h>
#include<conio.h>
#include<math.h>
#define m 8
#define pow_2_m 256

int main(){
        clrscr();

        int i,j,a[pow_2_m][m];

        ofstream out;
        out.open("G:\\thesis\\code\\addition\\s_in.in",ios::out);

        for(i=0;i<pow_2_m;i++){

        a[i][0]=fmod((i/pow(2,7)),2);
        a[i][1]=fmod((i/pow(2,6)),2);
        a[i][2]=fmod((i/pow(2,5)),2);
        a[i][3]=fmod((i/pow(2,4)),2);
        a[i][4]=fmod((i/pow(2,3)),2);
        a[i][5]=fmod((i/pow(2,2)),2);
        a[i][6]=fmod((i/pow(2,1)),2);
        a[i][7]=fmod(i,2);

        }

        for(i=0;i<pow(2,m);i++)

        {for(j=0;j<m;j++)
         out<<a[i][j]<<" ";
         out<<"\n\n";
        }
```

Appendix

```cpp
        getch();
        return 0;
    }
// TCP Sender Generation

#include<fstream.h>
#include<conio.h>
#include<math.h>
#include<stdlib.h>
#define m 8
#define r 4

int xor(int a,int b){
        return (a&&(!b)||(!a)&&b);
}

int main(){
        clrscr();

        char ch;
        int i,j,k,l,a[m+r],d[m],ri,rd[r],change_bit_position;

        int rb[r][10]={
                {1,3,5,7,9,11},
                {2,3,6,7,10,11},
                {4,5,6,7,12},
                {8,9,10,11,12}
        };

        ifstream s_in;
        s_in.open("G:\\thesis\\code\\sender\\s_in.in",ios::in);

        ofstream s_out;
        s_out.open("G:\\thesis\\code\\sender\\s_out.in",ios::out);

        ofstream r_in;
        r_in.open("G:\\thesis\\code\\sender\\r_in.in",ios::out);
```

Appendix

```
for(l=0;l<pow(2,m);l++){

s_out<<"Message["<<l<<"]: ";

for(i=m-1;i>=0;i--)
        {s_in>>d[i];
        s_out<<d[i]<<" ";
        }
        s_out<<"   ";


j=0;ri=0;
for(i=0;i<m+r;i++){
        if(i!=pow(2,ri)-1){
                a[i]=d[j];
                j++;
                continue;
        }
        ri++;
}


ri=0;
for(i=0;i<m+r;i++){
        if(i==pow(2,ri)-1){
                rd[ri]=0;
                for(j=1;rb[ri][j]!=NULL;j++)
                        rd[ri]=xor(rd[ri],a[rb[ri][j]-1]);
                a[i]=rd[ri];
                ri++;
        }
}

s_out<<"   Hamming Code["<<l<<"]: ";


if(l%2==1)
```

Appendix

```
        change_bit_position=random(12);
        cout<<" "<<change_bit_position;


for(i=m+r-1;i>=0;i--)
        {s_out<<a[i]<<" ";

        if(l%2==1 && i==change_bit_position)
        r_in<<xor(1,a[i])<<" ";

        else

        r_in<<a[i]<<" ";

        }
        s_out<<"\n\n";

        r_in<<"\n\n";

} //end 1st for

        getch ();
        return 0;
}
```

****

Appendix C

```
****Perl Code to count packets from Trace file****
                $infile=$ARGV[0];
                $tonode=$ARGV[1];
                $granularity=5;
                    $sum=0;
                open (DATA,"<$infile")
                || die "Can't open $infile $!";
```

Appendix

```perl
while (<DATA>)
    {
    @x = split(' ');

    if ($x[0] eq 'r' )
        {
        if ($x[3] eq 4 )
            {
            if ($x[4] eq 'tcp' )
                {
                $sum=$sum+1;
                }
            }
        }
    }

print STDOUT "$sum\n";

close DATA;
exit(0);
```

****

****Perl Code to calculate amount packets per unit time****

```perl
$throughput=0;
$sum=0;
$clock=0;

open (DATA,"<$infile")
    || die "Can't open $infile $!";

while (<DATA>)
{
        @x = split(' ');
```

72

Appendix

```perl
if ($x[1]-$clock <= $granularity )
{
if ($x[0] eq 'r' )
{
if ($x[3] eq $tonode )
{
if ($x[4] eq 'tcp' )
{
$sum=$sum+$x[5];
}
}
}
}

else
{
        $throughput=$sum/$granularity;
        print STDOUT "$x[1] $throughput\n";
        $clock=$clock+$granularity;
        $sum=0;
}
}

        $throughput=$sum/$granularity;
        print STDOUT "$x[1] $throughput\n";
        $clock=$clock+$granularity;
        $sum=0;

        close DATA;
        exit(0);
```

****

Bibliography

[1] Nayama Islam, Sumyea Helal, "Performance Analysis of TCP Tahoe, Reno, New Reno and SACK over Cellular Mobile System", 8th ICCIT 2005,page 786 to 790, Department of Information and Communication Technology, University of Rajshahi, Rajshahi-6205, Bangladesh.

[2] NS, The network simulator-ns-2.27.URL:http://www.isi.edu/nsnam/ns

[3] Benyuan Liu, DennisL.Goeckel and Don Towsley, "TCP-Cognizant Adaptive Forward Error Correction in Wireless Networks", Department of Computer Science, University of Massachusetts, Department of Electrical and Computer Engineering, University of Massachusetts.

[4] Paul Meeneghan and Declan Delaney, "An Introduction to NS, Nam and OTcl scripting" National University of Ireland.

[5] Jae Chung and Mark Claypool, "NS by Example".

[6] "NS Simulator for beginners", Lecture notes, 2003-2004, Univ. de Los Andes, Merida, Venezuela and ESSI, Sophia-Antipolis, France, December 4, 2003.

[7] "ns Tutorial", http://www.isi.edu/nsnam/ns/tutorial/nsindex.html

[8] "The ns Manual", The VINT Project, A Collaboration between researchers at UC Berkeley, LBL, USC/ISI, and Xerox PARC. December 13, 2003.

[9] Tanja Lang, "Evaluation of different TCP versions in non-wireline environments", The University of South Australia, Institute for Telecommunications Research, 31 August 2002.

74

[10] Minna Kaisa and Juonolainen, "Forward Error Correction in INSTANCE",UNIVERSITY OF OSLO, Department of Informatics.

[11] Johanna Antila, "TCP Performance Simulations Using Ns2", e-mail: jmantti3@cc.hut.fi.

[12] Henrik Lindquist and Gunnar Karlsson, "TCP with end-to-end FEC", In Proceedings of International Zurich Seminar on Communications, pages 152 – 155, Zurich, Switzerland, February 2004.

[13] Hasegawa, Kenji Kurata and Masayuki Murata "Analysis and Improvement of Fairness between TCP Reno and Vegas for Deployment of TCP Vegas to the Internet", Graduate School of Engineering Science, Osaka University.

[14] Fall K. and Floyd, "Simulation based comparison of Tahoe, Reno, and Sack TCP ", Computer Communication Review, Vol. 26, No. 3, July 1996, pp. 5-21.

[15] Lakshman, V, and Madhow, "The performance of TCP\IP for Networks with high Bandwidth Delay Products and Random loss", U. IEEE/ACM Transaction On Networking, Vol. 5, No.3, June 1997.

[16] Michele Zorzi, A. Chockalingam, and Ramesh R. Rao, "Throughput Analysis of TCP on Channels with Memory", Senior Member, IEEE.

[17] Claudio Casetti, MarioGerla, Scott Seongwook Lee, Saverio Mascolo and Medy Sanadidi, "TCP WITH FASTER RECOVERY", Computer Science Department, University of California, LosAngeles, USA.

[18] Hari Balakrishnan, Venkata N. Padmanabhan, Srinivasan Seshan, and Randy H. Katz, "A Comparison of Mechanisms for

Improving TCP Performance over Wireless Links", Student Member, IEEE.

[19] HALA ELAARAG, "Improving TCP Performance over Mobile Networks", Stetson University.

[20] Ling-Jyh Chen, Tony Sun, M. Y. Sanadidi, Mario Gerla, "Improving Wireless Link Throughput via Interleaved FEC", UCLA Computer Science Department, Los Angeles, CA 90095, USA {cclljj, tonysun, medy, gerla}@cs.ucla.edu.

[21] V. Jacobson, "Congestion Avoidance and Control", Computer Communication Review, vol. 18, no. 4, pp. 314--329, Aug. 1988. ftp://ftp.ee.lbl.gov/papers/conga-void.ps.Z.

[22] M. Miyoshi, M. Sugano and M. Murata, "Performance evaluation of TCP throughput on wireless cellular networks", IEEE Vehicular Technology Conference (VTC) 2001, vol.3, 2001, pp.2177–2181.

[23] J. Mo, R.J. La, V. Anantharam, J. Walrand, "Analysis and comparison of TCP Reno and Vegas", IEEE INFOCOM '99, Conference on Computer Communications, vol.3, 1999, pp.1556—63.

[24] A.S. Tannenbaum, Computer Networks, Prentice Hall, 3 edition, 1996.

[25] T. Kim, S. Lu, V. Bharghavan, "Improving congestion control performance through loss differentiation", Proceedings Eight International Conference on Computer Communications and Networks IEEE. 1999, pp.412—18.